Easy Piano

POPULAR CLASSICAL SONGS

The Friendly Way to Learn to Play the Classics

Arranged by
BRYSON WALKER

NOW ON

To view to a performance of these songs please visit our YouTube channel

https://youtu.be/AS8X8AS8dG8

(or simply search Walkercrest Easy Piano Popular Classical Songs)

 Walkercrest

ISBN: 9798377950080

publishing@walkercrest.com

First Printing April 2023

Easy Piano
POPULAR
CLASSICAL
SONGS

The Friendly Way to Learn to Play the Classics

DEDICATION

For Wayne, Joy, Jannicke, Jarrus, Jesica, Maia, Logan, Lylah, Megan and Davin.

And to Leslie for her inspiration.

TO THE PIANIST

This collection is the most-friendly way for you to learn and play the classics.

The songs have been transposed so they have very few sharps and flats.

Although the music is simplified, great care has been taken to preserve the melody and harmony.

The ONE PAGE arrangements let you try them out to see if you want to learn the FULL version.

The FULL version gives you more of the composer's original music.

May playing these classics bring you great enjoyment as you impress and entertain your audience!

CONTENTS

ONE PAGE Arrangements

FULL Arrangements

Air

Johann Sebastian Bach

From Orchestral Suite No.3 Also known as "Air on the G String"

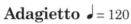

Fifth Symphony

Ludwig van Beethoven

From Symphony No. 5 in C Minor, Op. 67, Mvmt 1

Fur Elise

Ludwig van Beethoven

From Bagatelle No. 25 in A Minor

Con moto ♩ = 120

Ode to Joy

Ludwig van Beethoven

From Symphony No. 9, Op. 125, Mvmt 4

Habanera

Georges Bizet

From the Opera: Carmen Act I, No.5

Andante moderato ♩= 96

Lullaby

Johannes Brahms

From Wiegenlied, Op.49, No. 4

Etude

Frederic Chopin

From Etude Op. 10, No. 3 "Tristesse"

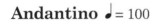

Andantino ♩ = 100

14

Fantaisie Impromptu

Frederic Chopin

From Fantaisie Impromptu, Op.66 in C# Minor

Allegretto ♩ = 112

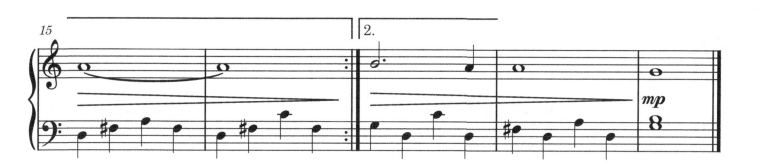

Clair de Lune

Claude Debussy

From Suite Bergamasque No.3

Andantino ♩ = 140

Reverie

Claude Debussy

17

Largo

Antonin Dvorak

From Symphony No. 9, Op. 95 "The New World" Mvmt 2

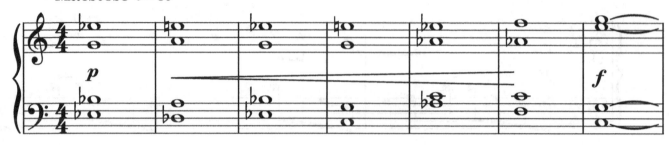

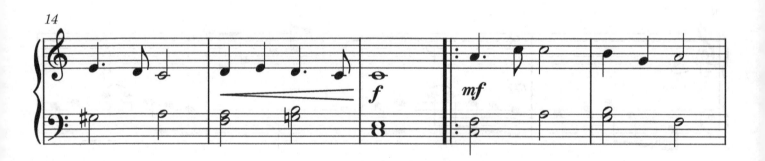

Pomp and Circumstance

Edward Elgar

From Pomp and Circumstance March No. 1 in D, "Land of Hope and Glory"

Grandioso ♩ = 88

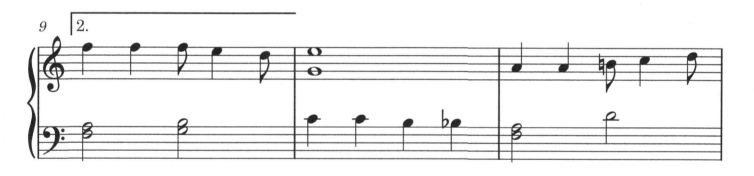

In the Hall of the Mountain King

Edvard Grieg

From Peer Gynt, Suite No. 1, Op. 46

Merry Widow Waltz

Franz Lehar

From the Operetta: The Merry Widow

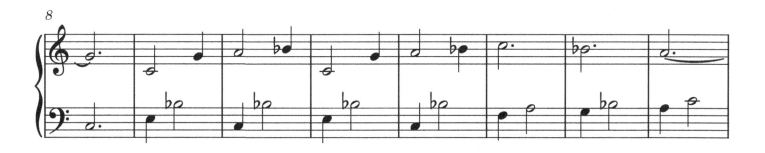

Eine Kleine Nachtmusik

Wolfgang Amadeus Mozart

From Serenade No.13 in G Major, K 525 "A Little Night Music"

Energico ♩ = 200

Can-Can

Jacques Offenbach

From the Operetta: Orpheus in the Underworld

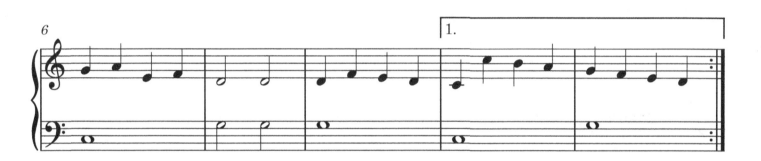

23

Tales of Hoffmann

Jacques Offenbach

From the Opera Fantastique: The Tales of Hoffmann

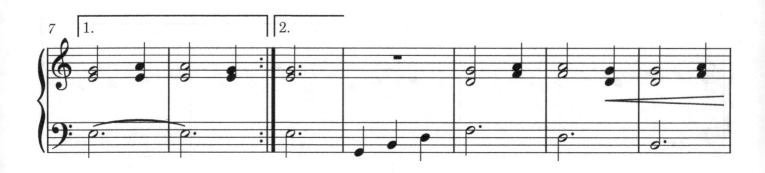

Canon

Johann Pachelbel

From Canon and Gigue in D Major, P 37

Bolero

Maurice Ravel

Song of India

Nikolay Rimsky-Korsakov

From the Opera: Sadko, Op. 5

Andante moderato ♩ = 112

William Tell Overture

Gioachino Rossini

From the Opera: Guillaume Tell

The Blue Danube

Johann Strauss II

From the Waltz: On the Beautiful Blue Danube, Op. 314

1812 Overture

Pyotr Ilyich Tchaikovsky

From The Year 1812, Solemn Overture, Op. 49

Romeo and Juliet

Pyotr Ilyich Tchaikovsky

From the Romeo and Juliet Fantasy Overture

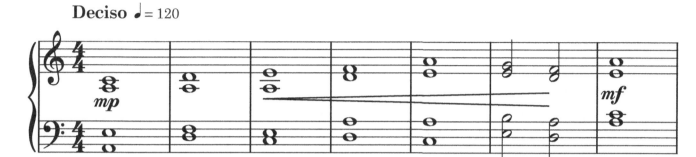

Swan Lake

Pyotr Ilyich Tchaikovsky

From the Ballet: Swan Lake, Op. 20

Andante moderato ♩ = 96

Four Seasons: Spring

Antonio Vivaldi

From the Concerto in E Major, Op. 8

Four Seasons: Summer

Antonio Vivaldi

From the Concerto in G Minor, Op. 8

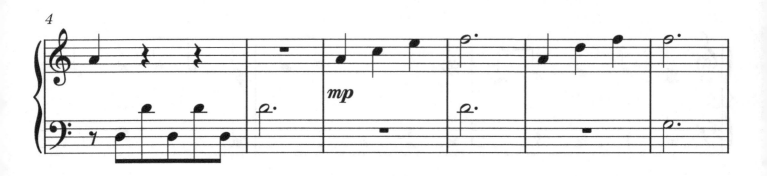

La Donna e Mobile

Giuseppe Verdi

From the Opera: Rigoletto

The Skaters Waltz

Emile Waldteufel

From Les Patineurs, Op. 138

FULL
Arrangements

of

Easy Piano
POPULAR
CLASSICAL
SONGS

Air

Johann Sebastian Bach

From Orchestral Suite No.3 Also known as "Air on the G String"

Air

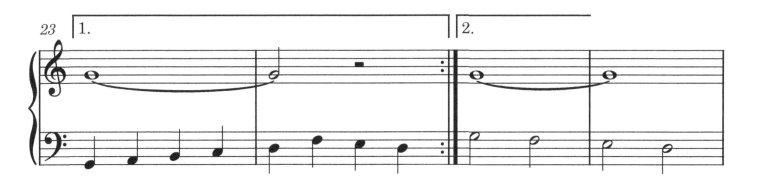

Air

Air

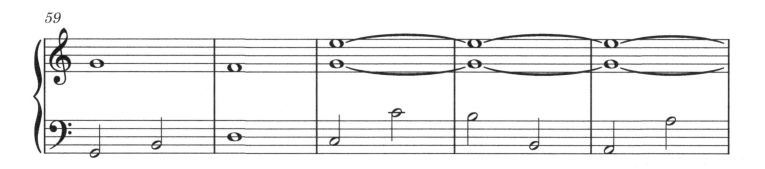

Fifth Symphony

Ludwig van Beethoven

From Symphony No. 5 in C Minor, Op. 67, Mvmt 1

Prestissimo ♩ = 200

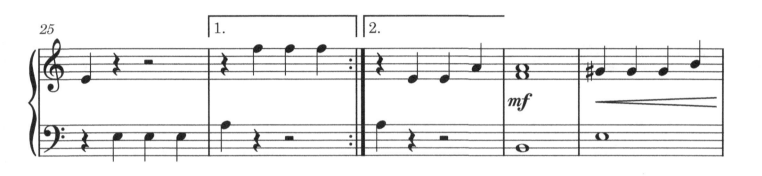

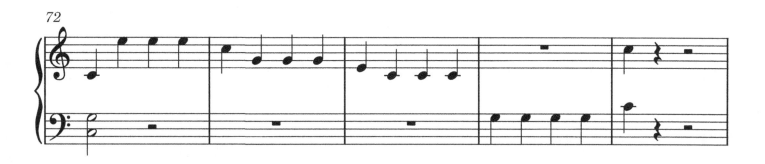

Fur Elise

Ludwig van Beethoven

From Bagatelle No. 25 in A Minor

Con moto ♩ = 120

Fur Elise

Ode to Joy

Ludwig van Beethoven

From Symphony No. 9, Op. 125, Mvmt 4

Ode to Joy

49

Habanera

Georges Bizet

From the Opera: Carmen Act I, No.5

Andante moderato ♩= 96

Lullaby

Johannes Brahms

From Wiegenlied, Op.49, No. 4

Andante ♩ = 80

Lullaby

Etude

Frederic Chopin

From Etude Op.10, No. 3 "Tristesse"

Andantino ♩= 100

Etude

Etude

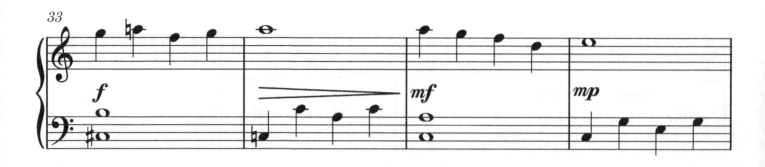

56

Fantaisie Impromptu

Frederic Chopin

From Fantaisie Impromptu in C# Minor, Op.66

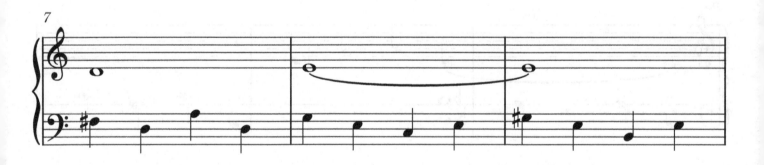

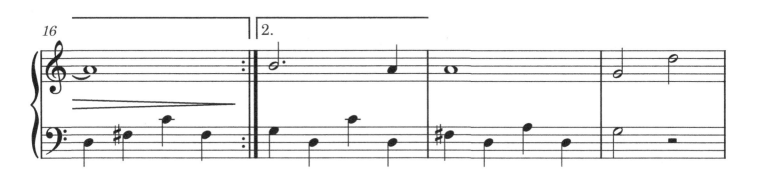

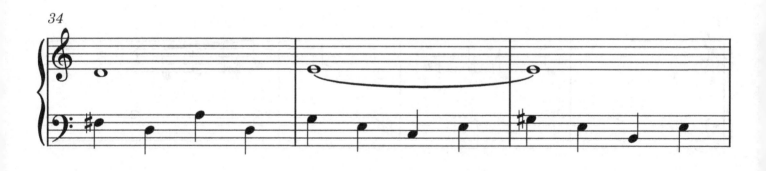

Fantaisie Impromptu

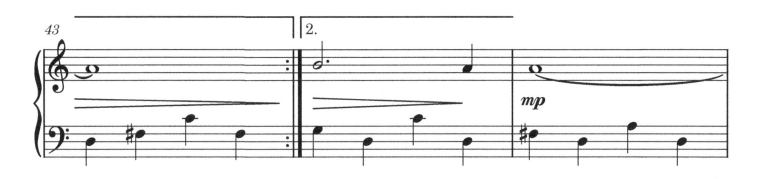

Clair de Lune

Claude Debussy

From Suite Bergamasque No.3 "Moonlight"

Andantino ♩ = 140

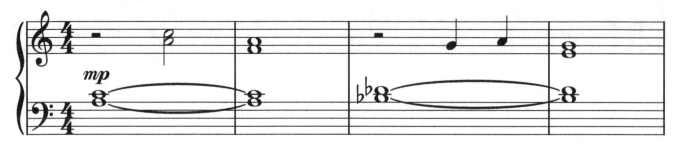

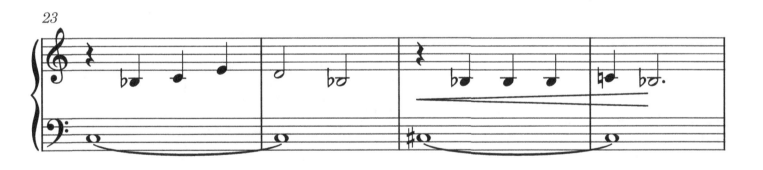

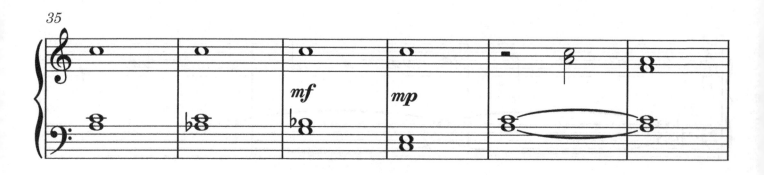

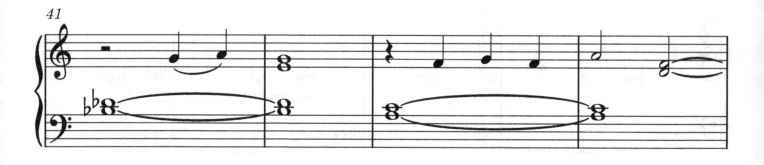

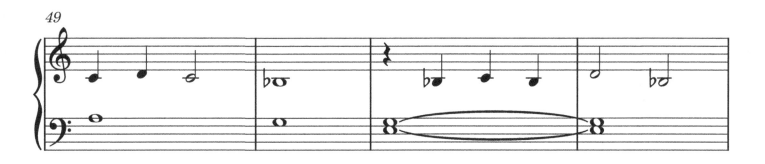

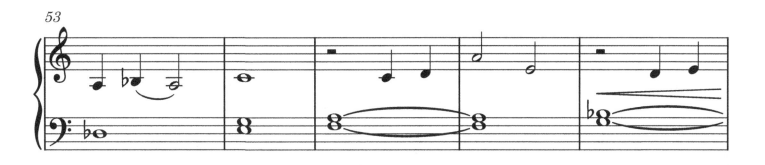

Reverie

Claude Debussy

Reverie

Reverie

68

Reverie

Largo

Antonin Dvorak

From Symphony No. 9, Op. 95 "The New World" Mvmt 2

Maestoso ♩ = 80

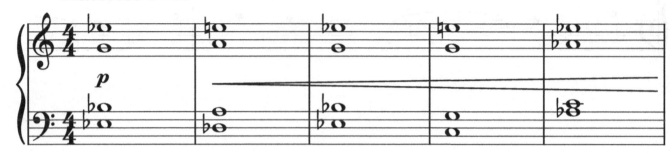

Largo

Largo

Largo

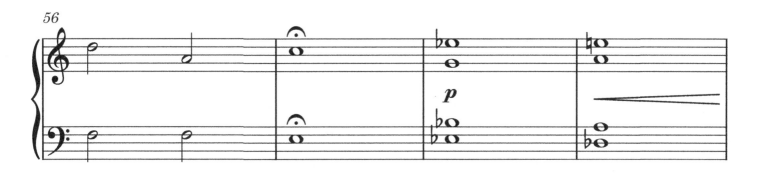

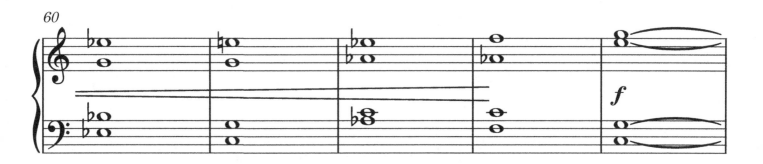

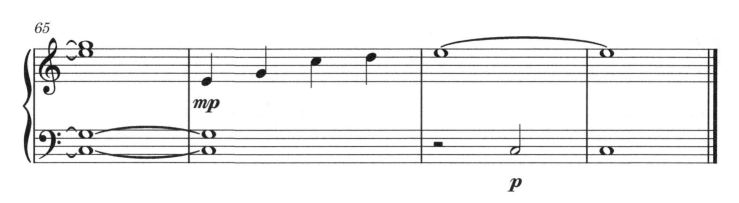

Pomp and Circumstance

Edward Elgar

From Pomp and Circumstance March No. 1 in D, "Land of Hope and Glory"

Pomp and Circumstance

75

In the Hall of the Mountain King

Edvard Grieg

From Peer Gynt, Suite No. 1, Op. 46

Merry Widow Waltz

Franz Lehar

From the Operetta: The Merry Widow

Energico ♩ = 144

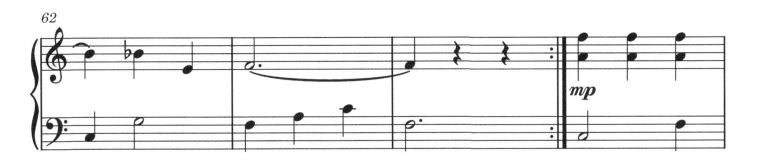

Eine Kleine Nachtmusik

Wolfgang Amadeus Mozart

From Serenade No.13 in G Major, K 525 "A Little Night Music"

Energico ♩ = 200

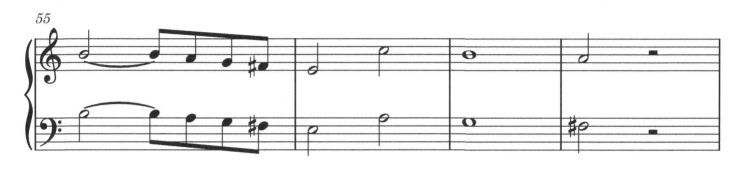

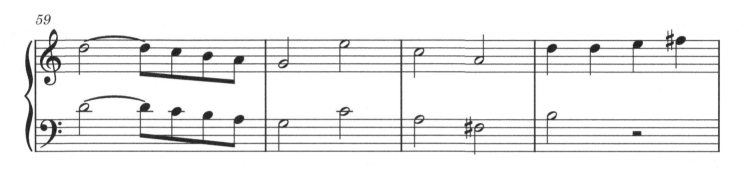

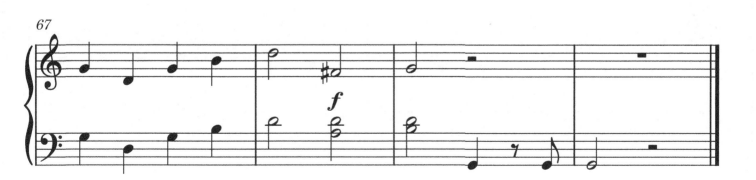

Can-Can

Jacques Offenbach

From the Operetta: Orpheus in the Underworld

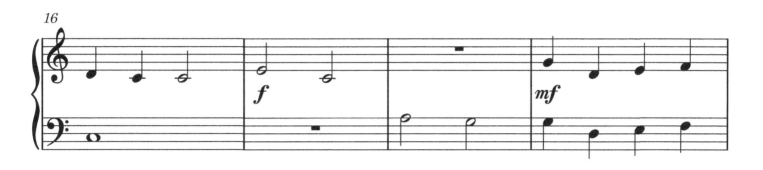

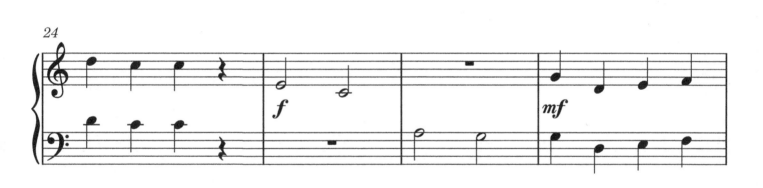

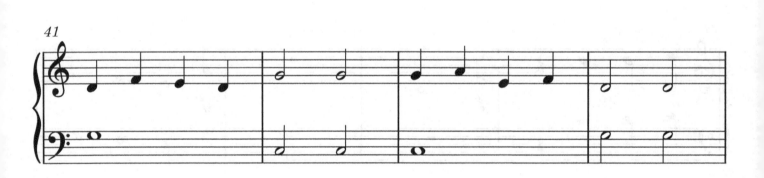

Can-Can

Tales of Hoffmann

Jacques Offenbach

From the Opera Fantastique: The Tales of Hoffmann

94

100

106

112

Canon

Johann Pachelbel

From Canon and Gigue in D Major, P 37

Con brio ♩ = 160

Canon

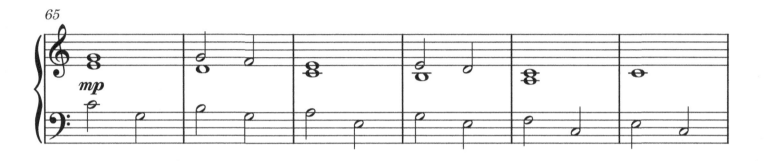

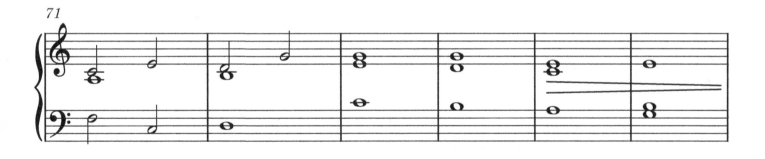

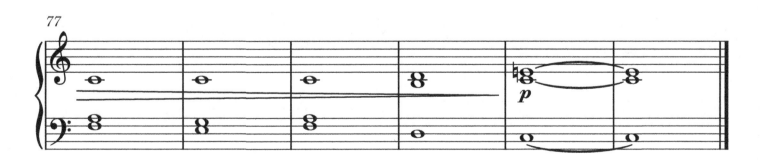

Bolero

Maurice Ravel

Bolero

Bolero

Bolero

Song of India

Nikolay Rimsky-Korsakov

From the Opera: Sadko, Op. 5

Andante moderato ♩ = 200

William Tell Overture

Gioachino Rossini

From the Opera: Guillaume Tell

Prestissimo ♩ = 200

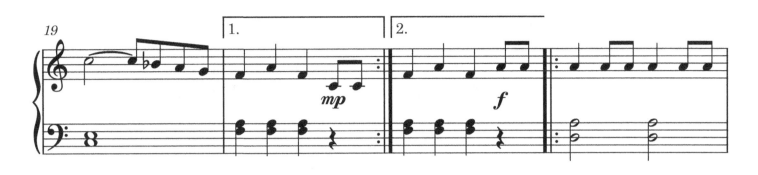

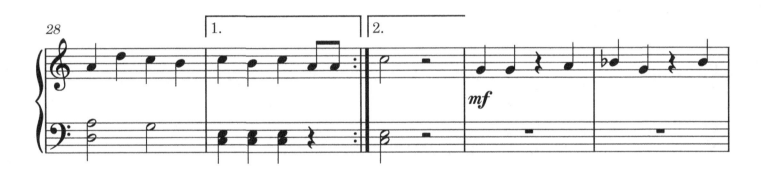

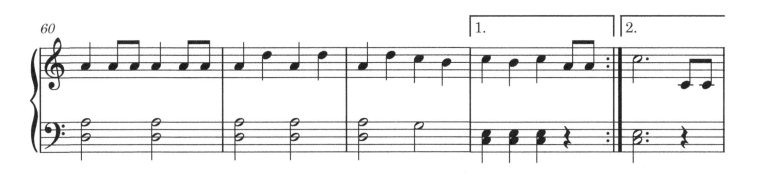

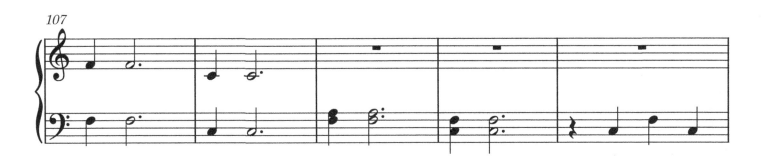

The Blue Danube

Johann Strauss II

From the Waltz: On the Beautiful Blue Danube, Op. 314

Vivace ♩ = 160

The Blue Danube

1812 Overture

Pyotr Ilyich Tchaikovsky

From The Year 1812, Solemn Overture, Op. 49

Marziale ♩ = 120

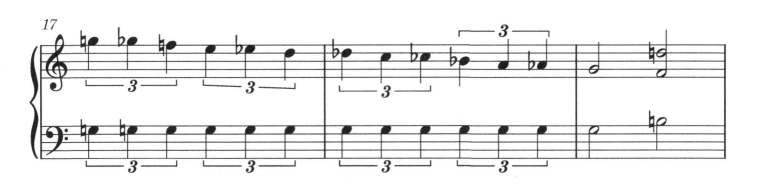

Romeo and Juliet

Pyotr Ilyich Tchaikovsky

From the Romeo and Juliet Fantasy Overture

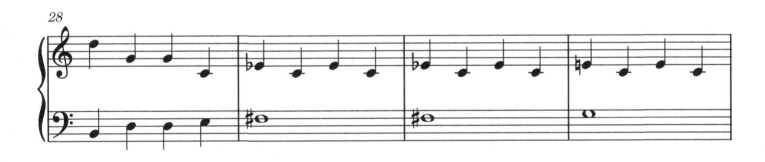

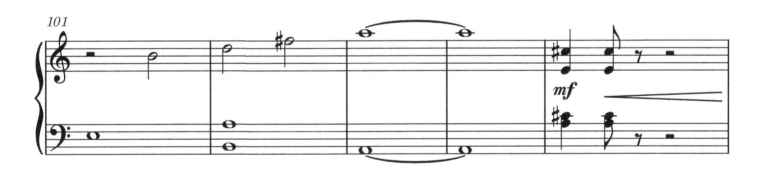

Swan Lake

Peter Ilyich Tchaikovsky

From the Ballet: Swan Lake, Op. 20

Four Seasons: Spring

Antonio Vivaldi

From the Concerto in E Major, Op. 8

Four Seasons: Summer

Antonio Vivaldi

From the Concerto in G Minor, Op. 8

La Donna e Mobile

Giuseppe Verdi

From the Opera: Rigoletto

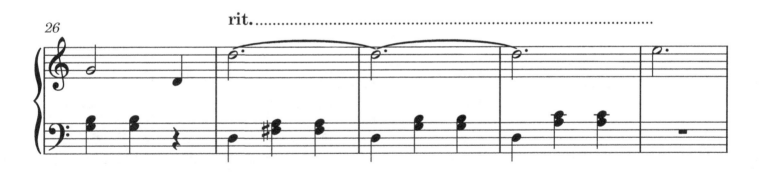

The Skaters Waltz

Emile Waldteufel

From Les Patineurs, Op. 138

Brillante ♩ = 172

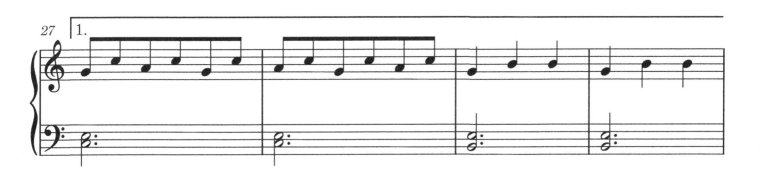

We hope you enjoyed playing these arrangements

More piano books are available from Walkercrest®

Super Easy Piano **Popular Classical Songs**

Super Easy Piano **Popular Classical Songs II**

Super Easy Piano **Hymns**

Super Easy Piano **Christmas Songs**

Super Easy Piano **Songs For Kids**

Super Easy Piano: **Bach**

Super Easy Piano: **Beethoven**

Super Easy Piano: **Chopin**

Super Easy Piano: **Debussy**

Super Easy Piano: **Mozart**

Super Easy Piano: **Strauss**

Super Easy Piano: **Tchaikovsky**

Super Easy Piano: **Vivaldi, The Four Seasons**

Easy Piano **Popular Classical Songs**

Easy Piano **Popular Classical Songs II**

Easy Piano **Christmas Songs**

Easy Piano **Hymns**

Easy Piano **Classical Love Songs**

Easy Piano: **Bach**

Easy Piano: **Beethoven**

Easy Piano: **Chopin**

Easy Piano: **Debussy**

Easy Piano: **Mozart**

Easy Piano: **Strauss**

Easy Piano: **Tchaikovsky**

Easy Piano: **Vivaldi, The Four Seasons**

Easy Piano: **New Age Music**

Intermediate Piano: **New Age Music**

Walkercrest also has music books for piano/vocal as well as other instruments and choirs.

About the Arranger

Bryson Walker received a Bachelor's Degree in Music Composition from Utah State University. He has composed and arranged music for the stage and the screen. Most recently he began teaching piano lessons to his grandchildren.

Finding a lack of classical music arranged for beginners, he set out to make these songs playable. "I really wanted to make these songs as friendly as possible while staying faithful to the original compositions," he said. "I hope my grandchildren and all pianists who want to play the classics will enjoy these simplified arrangements."

Please send any comments or suggestions to: publishing@walkercrest.com

Thank you for your patronage.

Made in United States
Orlando, FL
26 December 2024

56507511R00085